Sun

Everything I Never Told

You: A Novel

By Celeste Ng

: This is a quick read summary based on the book
"Everything I Never Told You: A Novel" by Celeste Ng

Note to Readers:

This is a Summary & Analysis of "Everything I Never Told You: A Novel" by Celeste Ng. You are encouraged to buy the full version.

TABLE OF CONTENTS

Thought-provoking Moments

Prequels/Sequels

Final Analysis

SUMMARY/ANALYSIS

INTRODUCTION

Everything I Never Told You is a very different kind of mystery. It opens like countless other thrillers – a young girl vanishes from her home and is later found at the bottom of a lake, drowned. The town is shocked and fascinated by the tragedy, and the police launch an investigation. But as the mystery unfolds, we find that the clues to Lydia Lee's untimely demise are embedded deep within the history of the girl's family.

At first, the Lees seem like the perfect all-American clan, with sixteen-year-old Lydia as the flawless, favored child. However as the Lees mourn and desperately search for answers, the ugly truth of the pursuit of perfection is revealed. The Lees are mixed-race Chinese and white family and in 1977 small town Ohio, they stick out like a sore thumb. Lydia's parents, James and Marilyn each carry deep regrets – James always longed to fit in and have friends, and Marilyn dreamt of being among the ranks of the first woman doctors in America, before pregnancy and marriage dashed her ambitions. So instead they turned their hopes and expectations on Lydia, forcing her to resort to lies and deception to keep them happy. Meanwhile, their other children, Nath and Hannah, watched from the fringes, knowing they would never have their parents' full attention. But Nath knew that Lydia was buckling under the pressure – and something had to give.

This novel bounces back and forth in time, detailing the investigation in Lydia's death alongside the Lee's backstory. Each of the remaining family members is keeping secrets from the others, and each holds a piece of the puzzle. Don't expect a stereotypical thriller with this book. Instead, Celeste Ng beautifully reveals the struggle of new kind of family desperately seeking acceptance in America, as well as the darker side of parental pride and ambition. This is a highly entertaining and thought-provoking read that will linger in your mind long after you put it down.

SETTING

The bulk of the story takes place in 1977 in a fictitious small college town in Ohio. This is the idyllic setting for the perfect all-American family – and the place that neither James nor Marilyn ever wanted to be. James planned to teach at Harvard, while Marilyn scorned domestic duties and dreamt of becoming a doctor. However, prejudice and pregnancy forced their hand and the Lees ended up making their home in Middlewood, just off the lake – the lake where Lydia's body would eventually be found.

The setting is critical to the plot of this novel because the atmosphere of 1977 Middlewood affectively serves to isolate the Lees, as the only non-white family in town. With their own ambitions unrealized and their lives unsatisfying, Marilyn and James have way too much time on their hands to focus on pressuring Lydia to achieve. In many ways the setting serves as a crucible – forcing the Lees together. Nath and Lydia both feel trapped, and both search for a way out.

PLOT ANALYSIS

The story is told in the third person omniscient point of view, with the reader able to flit in and out of the heads of the Lee family. This creates a wonderful sense of dramatic irony throughout the novel, as the reader learns the secrets that each of the characters are keeping from the others. However readers should pay close attention because every once in a while it can be difficult to know whose thoughts we are following at a particular given moment.

The novel has twelve chapters, each divided into several sections. The novel continuously flashes backward and forward in time, but for the most part, each chapter remains limited to a specific period in time. Ng deftly handles the transitions and the timing is never muddled.

HOW TO USE THIS SUMMARY

The rest of this summary is divided into two parts. Part One contains a brief character guide and a chapter by chapter breakdown. Each section contains a summarization of the grouping, interspersed with analytical comments. Part One is designed to be read <u>alongside </u>the novel. Therefore, each section only contains spoilers for that chapter, although there may be vague hints about what to look for as you continue to read. Part Two discusses the novel and its themes overall, and is designed to be read <u>after</u> completing the novel. Therefore it will contain spoilers about the book's ending.

PART ONE

Character Guide:

Main Characters

Lydia Lee: Sixteen-year-old daughter of Marilyn and James. Her death is the focal point of the novel. She strived to be the perfect daughter to both her parents, but chafed under their demanding expectations.

Marilyn Lee: Lydia's mother. Blonde, Caucasian. She is extremely intelligent and dreamed of being among the first woman doctors in America, but was forced to leave school when she met James and became pregnant. She pushes Lydia to become a doctor.

James Lee: Lydia's father. American born to Chinese immigrants. Professor of American history. He was the only Chinese boy in his school and never fit in among his peers. He pushes Lydia to be social and make lots of friends.

Nathan "Nath" Lee: Lydia's older brother. He is about to leave to attend Harvard College. He is Lydia's closest confidante, but also resents her for being the center of attention in the household. He is very intelligent and passionate about space exploration.

Hannah Lee: Lydia's younger sister. She has been largely ignored by her parents all her life, since they focused their attention on Lydia. She tries desperately to be included in her family's lives. Because of her frequent isolation, she is very observant.

Secondary Characters:

Jack Wolff: The Lee's neighbor. He is Nath's age and is rumored to be a wild child. Nath hates him, but in the months leading up to her death, Lydia had become fascinated with him. Nath believes he has something to do with Lydia's death.

Louise Chen: James' teaching assistant. She is drawn to James because he is also Chinese.

Marilyn's mother: A home economics teacher who expected Marilyn to grow up and become a perfect housewife. She disapproved of Marilyn's marriage to James.

Officer Fiske: The lead policeman assigned to Lydia's case. He is very kind, but James resents him because he perceives that Officer Fiske is prejudiced against the Lees for being a mixed-race family.

Dr. Janet Wolff: Jack's mother. Marilyn both admires her and is jealous of her for being such a highly respected woman doctor.

CHAPTER SUMMARIES/ANALYSES

CHAPTER ONE

Sixteen-year-old Lydia Lee is dead. This is the absolute first thing we learn in chapter one and the rest of the chapter is devoted to the events that lead up to the discovery of her body. It is May 3, 1977 in Middlewood. Nath, Lydia's older brother, and Hannah, her younger sister, are eating breakfast, when her mother, Marilyn first realizes that she is missing. Her bed has not been slept in all night. After Nath and Hannah leave for school, Marilyn reflects on Lydia's tendency to keep secrets. She calls Lydia's school and learns that her daughter has not arrived at school. Horrible thoughts begin to run through Marilyn's mind – stories of children who were kidnapped and murdered. It is a tense time in America, with Son of Sam just starting his reign of terror in New York City. Marilyn decides to call Lydia's father.

James Lee is grading papers in his office – he is a professor of American History at the local college. His teaching assistant, Louise Chen, comes into his office. James plucks something from Louise's hair – a gesture that causes her to blush. Another professor, Stanley Hewitt, whom James dislikes, interrupts the charged moment. He makes a smug remark about Louise's beauty to James when the pair are alone, which angers James. But before he can dwell on it, he receives the call from Marilyn, who asks him to come home.

The Lee family watches as the police search Lydia's room for clues. The police are not overly concerned – they believe Lydia has run away and will come home before long. A brief exchange between an officer and James reveals to us that Marilyn had gone missing 11 years earlier – but James insists that was simply a misunderstanding. The police take a photo of Lydia to distribute and advise James and Marilyn to call her friends. Nath listens as his parents call three girls who Lydia refers to as her best friends, but privately he knows that they are just girls who bully Lydia into giving them answers to homework. Nath knows that Lydia has been hanging out with a neighbor – a wild boy named Jack – lately, but doesn't tell his parents because he fears their reaction to finding out he hadn't told them sooner. He remembers that he hadn't paid Lydia any attention the night before.

Meanwhile, Hannah also thinks back to the night before. She had been unable to sleep, and in the middle of the night she looked out her window to see Lydia sneaking out. She wonders if she should tell her parents what she saw, but she also fears their anger.

The next day, a rowboat is discovered drifting in the middle of the town lake/swimming hole. The police ask James if Lydia had ever used it and he says never – she was afraid of swimming.

On Thursday, the police drag the lake and find Lydia's body.

CHAPTER TWO

This chapter tells the story of James' and Marilyn's relationship. Marilyn's backstory is the tale of a young woman in 1950s America trying her hardest to avoid convention and to become something more than a housewife. Her own mother had strived to be the picture-perfect housewife even after Marilyn's father left the family. But Marilyn wanted to take shop class instead of home economics. She scored the highest grades in her class in the sciences. And when she won a scholarship to Radcliffe, she told her skeptical advisor that she was going to become a doctor – not a nurse.

However, in her junior year, Marilyn met James Lee – her professor for a history elective. She was intrigued – he was the first Chinese man she had ever known and his mannerisms were completely different from other boys who had been interested in her before. After class, she visited him in his office and impulsively kissed him. She ended up dropping the class and she and James became lovers.

James fell in love with Marilyn because she made him feel like he belonged for the first time in his life. His own parents had immigrated to the United States at a time when discrimination against the Chinese was rampant and they struggled to find decent job. They took work at a school in Iowa because James would be able to study there for free. James was the first Oriental in his class, and struggled with isolation from his classmates throughout his entire education. He studied American history and culture obsessively in order to try and fit in, but it didn't help feel included. So when Marilyn showed an interest, he fell for her almost instantly.

James and Marilyn's relationship caused both of them to make small changes for each other – James started dressing differently and Marilyn showed off her domestic side by cooking for him. However they both retained their ambitions – until life took an unexpected turn. Harvard declined to hire James as a full professor and Marilyn got pregnant. So they moved to Ohio and got married.

Marilyn's mother didn't approve of James and tried several times to persuade her daughter not to marry him. This was a time period in which the struggle for acceptance of interracial marriages in America was a hot topic. Marilyn ignored her mother's protests and married James anyway. She never saw her mother again.

CHAPTER THREE

This chapter details what each member of the Lee family experiences on the day of Lydia's funeral. Nearly everyone in town shows up, but not because they knew Lydia or the rest of the Lee family well – they are interested in the spectacle of a murder.

Nath sees Jack at the funeral and is filled with anger. He confronts Jack afterward and tells him that he knows Jack knows something about Lydia's death that he isn't telling. Jack seems genuinely bewildered and James scolds Nath for fighting. Nath is still suspicious. Jack makes a game of taking girls' virginities and Nath doesn't trust him. Later, Nath eavesdrops while Officer Fiske question Jack. Jack tells them that he was with Lydia the afternoon she disappeared, but that he didn't see her after that. He says that Lydia was upset about a lot of things, but he doesn't know what could have happened to her.

Marilyn is angry with James for insisting on a closed

casket. After the funeral, she disappears into her room. Later she visits Lydia's room, searching for some clue about what happened to her. She notices that Lydia has kept all the decorations her mother has given her over the years, and remembers how she was fixated on becoming a doctor like Marilyn wanted to be. Marilyn wonders if her daughter's diaries will tell her the secrets that Lydia kept, but all the diaries are blank. Marilyn makes a vow to catch her daughter's killer.

James insisted on a closed casket because Lydia's face had been partially eaten away, but he cannot bring himself to tell that to Marilyn. After the funeral, he goes to his office and reads Lydia's autopsy report. He is repulsed by the gruesome details, but cannot stop reading it. The autopsy revealed that Lydia died from drowning. Louise comes into his office. She invites him to her apartment for lunch, but when they get there, she immediately takes him into the bedroom and they have sex. Afterward, he falls asleep in her apartment – the first deep sleep since Lydia's body was discovered. He wakes up in the middle of night and leaves for home.

Hannah wants to comfort her family, but no one has paid any attention to her throughout the day. She wishes her mother would comfort her.

CHAPTER FOUR

This chapter flashes back to eleven years before – when Marilyn went missing. Nath was in first grade and Lydia was in nursery school and Marilyn found herself with free time on her hands for the first time since she got pregnant. She started to think about going to school again or finding a job, but wasn't confident that she would be able to do it. Then she met a chemistry professor named Tom Lawson at the university Christmas party and asked for a job as a research assistant. But James, afraid that people would think he could not support his family, refused to let Marilyn take the job.

Four months later, Marilyn received word that her mother had died. She drove home to settle her mother's estate and discovered her mother's old cookbook. Her mother had penciled in notes about the satisfaction of being a good housewife. Marilyn becomes terrified at the thought that she will end up like her mother – remembered for nothing but her domestic chores. She vows not to let that happen.

Meanwhile, James experienced his first disappointment in his son. He had taken Nath to the YMCA and forced him to play with other kids in the pool. The other kids, including Jack, had played a cruel prank on Nath and Nath took it badly. James was painfully reminded of his own youth, when teachers would look the other way as children bullied him.

When Marilyn arrives home, she stops cooking and being domestic. She tries to get the research assistant job but it is no longer available. Full of despair, she goes to the hospital just to watch the doctors. There, she see Jack's mother, Dr. Wolff. She realizes that being a woman doctor is not such an impossible dream after all. Full of renewed vigor, she enrolls in a nearby community college, and starts to plan to leave her family. She is extra loving and attentive, and prepares delicious meals for them to have something to eat after she leaves. She contemplates leaving a note, but in the end she decides it would be better if she just disappeared.

CHAPTER FIVE

This chapter takes place nearly a month after Lydia's death. For three weeks, Hannah has been practicing how to sneak out of the house. She wants to retrace her sister's steps the night she disappeared. She creeps out of the house in the dead of night and walks to the lake. There she sits – thinking about the summers the Lee family spent by the water and wondering what happened to Lydia. Then she returns home and goes into Lydia's room. She falls asleep in her sister's bed and decides to do the same thing every night.

The next morning, Marilyn and James argue – Marilyn is upset that James is not more worried about the door being unlocked all night. (Hannah did not lock the door when she returned.) Marilyn believes that Lydia was taken from the house, but James does not agree. He is feeling guilty about his affair with Louise the day of the funeral.

Their argument is interrupted by the Officer Fiske. They have been investigating Lydia's school life and have discovered that she did not seem to have any friends. When they imply that Lydia might have committed suicide, both Marilyn and James respond with anger and disbelief. They interview Nath, who wonders if he should tell them about Jack, but again keeps it to himself. They ask him questions about Lydia's loneliness and if their parents ever harmed Lydia. Nath vehemently denies this, and then begins to cry, bringing the interview to an end.

Marilyn and James continue to fight. She accuses him of being too laidback and he leaves in anger. He drives around the lake and thinks about his relationship with Marilyn, and his continued affair with Louise. He cannot bring himself to break it off with her because when he is in her bed, he stops thinking about Lydia.

Meanwhile, Marilyn is furious that the police think Lydia committed suicide. She looks through her daughter's belongings and finds cigarettes and condoms hidden in the lining of Lydia's backpack. She realizes that she didn't know her daughter as well as she thought, and vows to figure out what other secrets she was keeping.

Hannah and Nath are at the lake when they see Jack coming down the street. Nath plans to confront him, but Hannah holds him back. Nath tells her he thinks Jack had something to do with Lydia's death. He also tells Hannah that Lydia had once fallen into the lake. Hannah just holds his hand – she is happy that someone in her family will finally let her get close to them.

CHAPTER SIX

This chapter flashes back again, to the summer that Marilyn disappeared. Nath and Lydia were bewildered, and every morning they expected their mother to have returned and life to be normal again. Officer Fiske told James that while they were looking for Marilyn, they don't think she will show up again unless she wants to. James found the note that Marilyn started to leave and then tore up, and kept it with him at all times. He struggled to care for the children, and did not know how to explain why their mother has disappeared.

A month after Marilyn disappeared, Nath snuck out of the house. He saw Jack on his porch and decided to go talk to him, even though Nath still held a grudge from the time Jack and the other kids had teased him. Jack tried to be friendly and comfort Nath over Marilyn's disappearance, but Nath became furious with him and ran off.

A few days later, the *Gemini 1* launched into space, and Nath became obsessed with all things astronaut, to avoid thinking about his mother. He tried to share his new love with his father, but James was reaching his breaking point, and one day he slapped Nath in the face to shut him up. He never hit him again, but from that point on, Nath kept his interest in space to himself. Lydia became obsessed with the thing that reminded her of her mother – the cookbook. She read the cookbook obsessively and vowed to be different if her mother would come back. She decided she would do anything her mother wanted.

Meanwhile, at college, Marilyn struggled to do her coursework while she misses her family. She repeatedly called home, but did not say anything when James answered the phone. Still she pressed on until one day she realized that she was pregnant. She visited the doctor – another woman doctor – who confirmed the pregnancy. The hospital got in touch with James, who was overjoyed to see Marilyn again. Marilyn realized that she would not be able to start medical school, and that once she returned home she would never be able to leave her family again.

When she returns home, Nath and Lydia were thrilled

to see her again. Lydia made good on her promise and did anything her mother asked – everything she could think of to make Marilyn happy. She told Marilyn that she destroyed her mother's cookbook, which makes Marilyn proud. Marilyn realized that while it might be too late for her to achieve her ambitions, Lydia could still make something more of herself. She started to push Lydia academically, drilling her on math and science.

One day, Marilyn and James went to clean out her apartment at college, leaving Nath and Lydia with a babysitter. Nath was feeling morose and neglected – his mother was almost completely ignoring him in her newfound quest to help Lydia learn. He sneaks out of the house and Lydia follows him, all the way to the lake. On a mad impulse, Nath pushed Lydia into the lake. He immediately regretted his decision and dove in to rescue her. They never told their parents, and ever since, Lydia had remembered that her brother saved her, while Nath remembered that he had pushed his sister into the lake.

Later that summer, the Lee family attended the elementary school's welcome back picnic. James and Nath entered the egg race and nearly won, but Nath tripped at the last minute. James made a snide remark that hurt Nath, and felt ashamed of himself for doing so. Nath and Lydia entered the three-legged race together, but got tangled up and fell to the ground.

CHAPTER SEVEN

This chapter flashes forward ten years – to the months leading up to Lydia's death. We learn that she became the center around which the Lee family revolved. Her father saw her as having the social life he never had. Her mother saw her as having the career she never had. The world was changing and women had more opportunities than ever. Marilyn expected Lydia is become a great doctor. Meanwhile, Nath knew that Lydia was miserable under the weight of their expectations – she made up lies about having friends, and fretted over her grades. Nath found himself unable to talk about his interests – his mother wasn't interested and his father didn't like to hear about space because it reminded him of the time he struck his son. Hannah was neglected from the moment she was born – put in an attic room and frequently forgotten.

At fifteen-and-a-half, Lydia was franticly hiding the fact that she was failing her classes from her parents. None of the science made any sense to her. She discovered her brother's acceptance letter to Harvard. Lydia had never managed to make friends. After Marilyn returned, Lydia was too preoccupied with making sure she didn't leave again and so she missed out on opportunities to spend time with other children. Nath was her only friend and he would be leaving her. She hid the acceptance letters from her brother.

Nath was fantasizing about escaping his family and studying the only subject that truly interested him – space. He had mixed feelings about leaving Lydia. On the one hand, he loved his sister. But on the other hand, he is sick and tired of living in a house where Lydia is unfailingly the center of attention. He became worried when he didn't receive his acceptance letter, but one day Jack gave him a letter that had been delivered to his house by mistake. Nath showed James and Marilyn, who are proud. Lydia watched their celebration, and then at that moment, she chose to tell them she was failing physics.

Throughout dinner that night, Marilyn berated Lydia for failing – warning her that if she doesn't correct the problem, she would never make anything of herself. Later, Lydia, her face worn and ashen, tried to apologize for Nath for ruining his moment, but he wouldn't let her.

All throughout Christmas break, Marilyn made Lydia study physics. Lydia hoped James would help her, but he never said anything to Marilyn. Nath was still angry with her and Hannah hid from everyone. Lydia became furious with them all.

On Christmas day, Lydia and Nath were starting to think about making up. Lydia dreaded getting another book from her mother, but was surprised and hopeful when James handed her a present instead. However she was disappointed to find that it was a book about how to make friends. She knew that it was something he wished he had when he was younger. She thinks back to the first time she pretended to have friends in order to make her father happy – she had been thirteen years old. Lydia read the book throughout that Christmas day, but grew more upset with every chapter. When Nath tried to cheer her up and take her picture, Lydia couldn't even muster up a smile.

After Christmas, Lydia went back to school and tried to do better in physics. She started to talk with Jack, who was also failing the class. Her parents kept badgering her about grades and friends. We learn that James, who was the one obsessed with Lydia having friends, had actually unknowingly sabotaged a potential friendship. Lydia tried to tell her parents about having befriended Jack. They did not react, but Nath was disturbed by the news. This spurred Lydia to decide to really become friends with Jack.

Lydia waited for Jack after school one day and asked for a ride. She tried to put on a fake persona for Jake, but saw right through it, taunting her about pretending to smoke and pretending not to care about physics. Still, Lydia persisted. The idea that her brother hated Jack and would be furious with her for spending time with him made her even more eager to get to know him. Jack started to respond to her more, and eventually they were on their way to becoming friends.

CHAPTER EIGHT

As the Fourth of July approaches, James tries to forget about his grief in two ways: he takes long drives and he finds his way into Louise Chen's bed. However, while Louise keeps his mind occupied for a short while, he finds himself increasingly angry and ashamed after each encounter. He entertains thoughts of suicide, and becomes increasingly irritated with his family, especially Nath. One day, he snaps at Nath, who responds in kind and insinuates that he knows about his father's affair. James physically grabs him and replies furiously, but regrets his outburst almost immediately. Nath doesn't speak to his father anymore, and leaves in anger.

The papers are still writing articles about Lydia's death. Her classmates and teachers keep talking about how much she stood out, and the reporters are beginning to speculate that the hardships of being a mixed-race girl became too much for her to bear. Just then James gets a call from Officer Fiske – they are closing the investigations and ruling it a suicide.

Marilyn does not take the news well. She still believes that someone lured Lydia to the lake, and she becomes furious when she thinks that James agrees with the police. She speculates that the police wouldn't have stopped investigating so soon if Lydia was white, and James fires back that if Lydia was white, she wouldn't have faced the hardships that the papers are speculating about. James leaves, and runs straight to Louise.

Louise comforts him and offers him traditional Chinese food that James has not had since his mother used to make it. They have sex, and James tells Louise that she is the type of girl he should have married. Internally, Louise hopes that he will leave his wife and marry her.

Marilyn tells Nath and Hannah what the police have decided. Nath is angry, and calls the police to persuade them to re-investigate Jack, but they dismiss his concerns. The Lees spend the rest of the day avoiding each other. Hannah spends her time looking at her treasures – little things she has stolen from her family over the years in order to feel closer to them. She thinks about Nath's suspicion of Jack, but she knows he is wrong. She remembers a day that she, Lydia and Nath spent at the lake the summer before. Jack had been there, and she observed from his behavior that he loved Nath, even though Nath hated him. Hannah recognizes a kindred spirit in Jack – someone desperate to be loved - and she knows he would never hurt anyone.

Marilyn is regretting her fight with James, and plans out what she will say when he gets home – that she never regretted marrying him. But he does not come home. When she starts to wonder if she should report him missing, Nath reluctantly tells her that he believes James is having an affair. Marilyn remembers Louise and drives to her apartment. James' car is in the parking lot. Louise is flustered to see her, and evades her questions about James, refusing to let Marilyn see into the apartment. Internally, Marilyn is enraged, but she stays deadly calm on the outside, asking Louise to send James home if she sees him.

CHAPTER NINE

Now we flash back to several months earlier, during Lydia's developing relationship with Jack. Nath was outraged at the thought of his sister spending time with a boy with a reputation for using girls and tossing them aside. But Lydia was thrilled with their relationship, because she has finally found someone to talk to. She was surprised when Jack wanted to know things about Nath, and that he seemed to want her to change Nath's opinion of him. Jack also started to teach her how to drive. Lydia realized that learning how to drive might permit her an escape for the first time in her life – she will be able to go wherever she wants.

At home, she balked when Marilyn starts harassing her about her schoolwork, but then she remembered how desperately she does not want to lose her mother again, so she acquiesced. That night, she tried to hide the letter inviting Nath to Harvard for his campus tour, but he discovered it and became angry with her, telling her to get used to the idea that he will soon be gone.

On her sixteenth birthday, James drove her to take her learner's permit test. Lydia was shocked and dismayed when Louise accompanied them, and believed from Louise's behavior that she and James were having an affair. This rattled Lydia so much that she did not complete her written driver's test and failed.

At home, Hannah was helping Marilyn make a birthday cake that looked like a driver's license. Hannah was thrilled to be included, but Marilyn didn't pay her much attention. When Lydia arrived home and told them she had failed, Marilyn frosted over the cake and they did not dwell on it. But Lydia new anger with her father, her continuing feud with Nath and her overall resentment of her mother caused her to be hostile during her birthday dinner. No one but Hannah seems to notice. Hannah realizes her sister is reaching some kind of breaking point, but she doesn't know how to help.

Chapter Ten

Flashing back to the present, James dresses and leave Louise's apartment. When he arrives home, Marilyn is still smoldering with a quiet rage, and scathingly tells him that he and Louise make a good couple. At first, James seems ready to silently take whatever Marilyn wants to say to him, but when she mentions her mother, he snaps. He tells Marilyn that she doesn't understand what it is like to always stick out – to never fit in. Marilyn fires back that she has faced plenty of harassment herself – at college the boys in her class did everything they could to try and get her to drop out. She realizes that James has always tried to get Lydia to fit into the crowd, while she always tried to get Lydia to stand out and rise above the crowd. Meanwhile Nath and Hannah crouch outside, listening to the entire conversation. James tells Marilyn to forget that she ever met him, and he flees. After he leaves, Nath takes the other car and leaves too.

Marilyn visits Lydia's room, and in a rage, she starts

destroying Lydia's things – all the science posters and books Marilyn had bought for her. She discovers her mother's cookbook tucked away in Lydia's room – Lydia had lied when she said she destroyed it. She remembers how Lydia loved to cook, and in despair she realizes how wrong she had been to try and force her own interests onto her daughter. A figure appears in Lydia's doorway, and for a moment Marilyn thinks it is Lydia. But it is Hanna. Marilyn embraces her remaining daughter.

Meanwhile Nath is getting drunk for the first time in his life. He buys two bottles of Fiskey and drives to the edge of town. But the Fiskey doesn't help him forget. He ends up vomiting out the side of the car. Officer Fiske discovers him and kindly takes him home.

As James drives, he feels impossibly torn. He longs to disappear like Marilyn did, but at the same time he cannot bear to leave his family. He thinks of Marilyn, lying among Lydia's things and mourning the daughter she had such big plans for. He wonders how he could have been so wrong.

Chapter Eleven

We flash back to right before Nath leaves for his campus visit. He was ecstatic to be leaving, while Lydia despaired. She watched Nath prepare and thought about when he would leave for good. She was torn – she wanted him to be happy and follow his passion for space, but she feared losing her one confidante. She made him promise he would call her while he was away.

Nath didn't call. Lydia waited for the phone to ring and tried to avoid Hannah, who shadowed her the entire time. Lydia noticed Hannah wearing a locket James had given her, and got angry. She slapped Hannah and ripped the locket from her, before calming down and telling her never to wear it again. Hannah was just happy to have Lydia paying attention to her.

That night, Lydia called Nath. He was annoyed to have his night interrupted, and when Lydia tried to tell him about her troubles at home, he snapped at her and mocked her for getting so upset about trivial things. He told her to go to Jack with her problems. Stunned and angry, Lydia decides to take his advice.

On Monday, the day she disappeared, Lydia put on her prettiest dress and went for a drive with Jack. She tried to initiate sex with him, but Jack did not respond. Jack tried to let her down gently, but Lydia, bewildered, insisted he tell her what the problem was. He revealed his feelings for Nath. Lydia was shocked and horrified to have been so wrong. She got angry and Jack snapped at her, telling her that at least he is not afraid to be himself. She left, threatening to tell Nath what she had learned. Back at home, she tried to pretend that nothing was wrong.

It worked. No one seemed to notice her mood at dinner. While she listened to Nath excitedly talking about his trip, she tried to figure out where her life had gone so wrong. She thought about what Jack said, and realized that he was right. She needed to stop being so afraid to stand up for herself and live her own life.

She decided to visit the lake to think everything over.

She left in the middle of night and went to the dock, thinking about all the things she had been afraid of in her life. She was afraid of losing people – her mother, her father and now Nath, the only person she felt truly understood her. She decided to make changes in her life – she would stand up to her mother and her father for the first time and start living her own life. She would apologize to Jack and try to be friends with him again. And she would let Nath go live his own life.

Lydia decided that as a metaphor for her new life, she should get over her fear of water. She rowed out in the rowboat, and was enchanted by the sight of the stars. She believed nothing was impossible for her. She stepped out into the water.

All this time, it was neither murder nor suicide, but simply a tragic accident. Lydia believed that if she wanted it bad enough, she could swim. She was wrong.

Chapter Twelve

Back to present day. James returns home, praying that he has not screwed things up for good. He finds Hannah curled up on the couch. She tells him she knew he would come home. James starts to feel happy for the first time. He puts Hannah on his back, like he used to do with Lydia and swings her around. But he doesn't use Hannah's name, he still calls out to Lydia. Hannah does not seem to mind. She is just happy to be with her father. When Marilyn comes downstairs and sends Hannah to bed so she and James can talk, Hannah goes to Lydia's room to sleep.

Without having to say much to each other, James and Marilyn decide they can work through it. James will not see Louise again. He and Marilyn will begin sharing the secrets they had kept from each other. James and Nath will eventually repair their relationship. They will all, as a family, start saying aloud how they feel about each other. For now, everything is fragile, but they are on their way to healing.

In the middle of the night, Marilyn wakes up. Taking care not to wake up James, who is beside her again, she visits Lydia's room. She is the grey area between wishing she could see her daughter one last time, and being ready to start moving on. She sees Hannah's sleeping form, and imagines that it is Lydia.

The next morning, Nath spots Jack outside walking his dog. He runs to confront him, with Hannah following close after him. Hannah tries to stop, to tell him that Jack had nothing to do with Lydia's disappearance. Jack tries to tell Nath the same thing, to say he's sorry about what happened, but he didn't do anything. Nath refuses to believe him. Jack realizes that Lydia hadn't told Nath about Jack's feelings for him. Nath just needs someone to hit. He punches Jack several times, and Jack doesn't even try to fight back. Nath realizes that it isn't making him feel better. He stops, turns and jumps into the lake.

He imagines letting himself drown, but instinct takes over and he kicks to the surface. He, Jack and Hannah go back to the Lee house and get patched up. The encounter has left them all physically dirty, but emotionally clean. It will take months or years before they fully recover from Lydia's death, but they are on their way to feeling happy again.

PART TWO

Alternate Endings

Everything I Never Told You ends on many hopeful notes – James and Marilyn are reconciling, Nath is finding the ability to work through the guilt he feels about Lydia's death, and Hannah is finally being seen and heard and loved as a daughter and a sister. Lydia's death has been ruled a suicide and only we know that it was actually an accident – the Lees will probably always suspect different things, but they will never be able to know for certain.

There are many ways in which the novel could have ended very unhappily. Towards the end, each of the Lees are volatile in their own way. James might have driven off and never come back, or he could have decided to leave Marilyn for Louise Chen. Marilyn could have become as obsessed with Lydia in death as she was obsessed with her in life, and abandoned her remaining family in order to search for an alternative explanation for her death. Nath's encounter with

Jack could have ended far more tragically, if he had not been able to stop himself from beating the other boy. And Hannah could have remained neglected and lonely, until she grew up to be bitter and self-destructive.

Celeste Ng weaves an improbable tale of a twisted family dynamic that is actually able to heal itself in the aftermath of a tragedy. It is a far cry from the stereotypical tale of a perfect family going to pieces and breaking apart after the death of a child. The novel might have ended dozens of other ways, but it would not have resonated in the same manner.

THEMES/SYMBOLS

Blending In Vs Standing Out

As a result of his race and his class, James is never able to fit in with his peers. He is bullied throughout school and faces varying levels of prejudice and insensitivity from his colleagues during his career. He longs to be able to blend in, and after he gives up on achieving this for himself, he focuses that ambition on his children. The first time Nath truly disappoints him is when he fails to fit in with the other kids. However Lydia is the "whitest looking" of his children, and she fools him into thinking she has made friends.

Meanwhile, Marilyn has always wanted to stand out, and when she realizes that she is doomed to be a housewife for the rest of her life, she also focuses her ambitions on Lydia. Because Lydia at first exhibits a high intelligence, and does anything she can to please her mother, Marilyn believes she will achieve what Marilyn could not.

Lydia is helplessly pulled between these two opposing forces. She also longs to be able to fit in with her siblings, but their parents' preference of her distances Lydia from Nath and Hannah. This is symbolized in the three-legged race that she and Nath attempt, soon after Marilyn returns from her summer away and begins to dote on Lydia. She and Nath end up helplessly tangled in each other – they are unable to work together.

Irony

Chapter two describes how Marilyn defined the word irony on an English test in high school as a contradictory outcome of events as if in mockery of the promise and fitness of things. This accurately describes many of the situations the characters find themselves in throughout the novel. Marilyn's mother tries her hardest to turn Marilyn into a domestic goddess, while Marilyn strives to become a scientist and a doctor. Then, in turn, Marilyn pushes Lydia relentlessly to pursue science, and discovers too late that Lydia had a propensity for cooking. The irony of Lydia's death is heartbreaking. Lydia decided to step into the water as a symbolic baptism of her new life and instead she drowned. And finally, Lydia's death brings a fractured family closer together, rather than driving apart as is the more expected outcome.

Escape

Almost every character in this book craves an escape of some kind. James wants to escape his own skin – his own race – in order to fit in with the crowd. Then later, he falls into an affair with Louise in order to escape his pain at losing Lydia. Marilyn quite literally escapes for a summer in order to go back to school. Nath cannot wait to go to Harvard to escape his family dynamic. And Lydia's disappearance and death are the result of her escape from the house one night. The novel exquisitely captures what it is like to feel trapped – by your family, by your circumstances and even by your own body. Perhaps this was the inspiration for setting the story in Ohio, and making Nath so fascinated in space. There is an old joke about the fact that Ohio has produced more astronauts than any other state – it is because people are so desperate to leave they will go to the moon if it means getting away.

REAL WORLD TRUTHS

While James and Marilyn represent a rather extreme case, the story of a child breaking under the weight of their parent's expectations in certainly not an unfamiliar one. When a parent holds their newborn in their arms, they are already envisioning his or her future, and it can be very hard to let go of that vision. Everyone has regrets about some part of their life, and it is all too easy for a parent to believe that their child can have "the life they never had." This is why you will see parents becoming much more invested in their child's activities than their child – why you see middle-aged men and women red-faced and screaming at referees and umpires. And when they are young, most children want nothing more than to please their parents. This is also why you see parents rejecting children who come out as gay or transgender. It can be next to impossible to let go of that vision of perfection. And children want to please their parents when they are young, but as they grow older, natural rebellion met with unrealistic expectations can often be a recipe for disaster.

Lydia's reaction to her mother's disappearance is also very natural – children of divorced parents often believe that the separation was their fault, and if they would only be good, their parents would be able to be together again. Lydia was so terrified of her mother leaving again that she went to heartbreaking lengths to convince Marilyn that she was the perfect daughter. Celeste Ng imbeds truths in her novel that every parent and child should pay attention to – we could all do with a reminder that our lives are our own to live, and that we should not expect anyone else to live up to impossible expectations.

THOUGHT-PROVOKING MOMENTS

This novel has much thought-provoking commentary on the harsh struggle of mixed-race families throughout the history of America, particularly the American Midwest. This is not an uncommon theme in literature, but Ng gives it a fascinating twist – how much of the Lee family's isolation is actually due to their unusual racial dynamic, and how much is due to a simple lack of social skills?

Yes, James did have a very difficult upbringing as the only Chinese person to attend his school, and he faced an amount of bullying that would make anyone reluctant to seek friendships. And yes, Marilyn's scorn of convention and her ambition to rise above the domestic life put her at odds with her peers. However it does seem strange that neither of them were able to make any friends in the 18 or so years that they lived in Middlewood, Ohio. At some point, the reader is forced to ask if James and Marilyn's isolation was partly self-inflicted – and if their failure to socialize ended up crippling their children when it came to making friends. After all, children learn social skills from their parents and other adults in their life, and James and Marilyn were the only adults in their children's lives. We even catch a glimpse of this when James inadvertently sabotages one of the only real chances Lydia has to make a friend at school.

It is also interesting to wonder if Lydia's grades would

have been so bad if she hadn't had such pressure on her. While it seems apparent that she would never have been the scientist or doctor that her mother wanted, she may have been better able to focus and concentrate if she wasn't so afraid of disappointing her mother. She might also have been less afraid to ask for help when she needed it.

PREQUELS/SEQUELS

The novel has its own prequel built in, with all the flashbacks to the Lee family history. However there is a lot of room for a sequel that explores the trials and tribulations the family goes through as they recover in the aftermath of Lydia's death. It is clear that they are not wholly convinced of the suicide explanation, and they will most likely never stop searching for answers. And while the novel ends on a hopeful note, with the implication that the Lee family is mending their relationship, it seem improbable that a family who existed for so long with such a twisted preoccupation with one child will easily transition into life without that child. There are even hints at the end of the novel that Marilyn and James will replace the hole Lydia left with Hannah – but this has some very disturbing implications as well. In one of the last scenes, James gives Hannah a piggyback ride, but pretends that she is Lydia. This might easily satisfy the affection-starved Hannah for a while, but eventually she may grow to resent her parents for it. And there are so many thrilling ways she could rebel against them.

A sequel might also explore a relationship between Nath and Jack, since there are hints in the final chapter that Nath might be able to return Jack's affection. This would certainly add a new layer to the isolation Nath faces as a mixed-race individual - the time period of the novel was both an exciting and terrifying one for gay men in America. And it would be very interesting – and potentially devastating – to see how James and Marilyn might react to the news that their son is gay.

Ng has created such a fascinating and disturbing group of characters that she could easily go on to create a compelling sequel.

FINAL ANALYSIS

Readers looking for a traditional mystery, or for non-stop action and thrills, may be disappointed in this novel – but just as likely, they may find themselves captivated by Celeste Ng's fascinating tale. This is a book that explores people's secret inner selves, and the things they keep from their loved ones. It is a hard hitting look at the perils of placing unrealistic expectations on your children, as well as the anguish caused when parents play favorites. And the final reveal of what happened to Lydia is devastating in its irony.

The best thing about this book is the way it leaves you still feeling somewhat unsettled at the end. The Lee family may have the appearance of being ready to move on and perhaps achieve a happily ever after – but appearances can be deceptive. And the Lee family is highly skilled at deception.

Made in the USA
San Bernardino, CA
10 November 2016